Delish Potato Salad Cookbook

Simple Potato Salad Recipes Excellent as Starter, Side Dish, or a Quick Dinner

BY: Allie Allen

COOK & ENJOY

Copyright Notes

This book is written as an informational tool. While the author has taken every precaution to ensure the accuracy of the information provided therein, the reader is warned that they assume all risk when following the content. The author will not be held responsible for any damages that may occur as a result of the readers' actions.

The author does not give permission to reproduce this book in any form, including but not limited to: print, social media posts, electronic copies or photocopies, unless permission is expressly given in writing.

My Gift to You for Buying My Book!

I would like to extend an exclusive offer to receive free and discounted eBooks every day! This special gift is my way of saying thanks. If you fill in the subscription box below you will begin to receive special offers directly to your email.

Not only that! You will also receive notifications letting you know when an offer will expire. You will never miss a chance to get a free book! Who wouldn't want that?

Fill in the subscriber information below and get started today!

https://allie-allen.getresponsepages.com/

Table of Contents

Easy and Delicious Potato Salad Recipes

sssssssssssssssssssssssssssssssssssssssssssss

1) Spicy Potato Salad

This mayonnaise-less potato salad is spicy but not to worry you can eliminate the spicy or tone it down to suit your taste.

Yield: 8

Cooking Time: 90 minutes

Ingredient List:

- Red potatoes (2lbs)
- Vinegar (¼ cup)
- Chili powder (1 ½ tsp.)
- Hot sauce (1/8 tsp.)
- Carrot (1, shredded)
- Green onions (4, sliced)
- Vegetable oil (1/3 cup)
- Sugar (1 tbsp.)
- Seasoned salt (1 tsp.)
- Canned corn (8 oz., whole kernel, drained)
- Ripe olives (2.5 oz., canned-sliced)

SSSSSSSSSSSSSSSSSSSSSSSSSSSSSSSSSSSSSSSSSSSSSSSSSSSS

Methods:

1. Heat water in saucepan (enough to cover potatoes); add potatoes to pan. Cook for 30 minutes or more until tender. Drain potatoes and put aside for 20 minutes to cool.

2. Cut cooled potatoes into cubes and place in a large bowl.

3. Combine oil with vinegar, sugar, chili powder, hot sauce and seasoned salt and add to potatoes. Toss to combine, cover and refrigerate for an hour.

4. Add corn, olives, carrots and scallion. Stir and serve.

2) All American Potato Salad

This All American Salad is definitely not high in fats as a traditional American potato salad. Canola mayonnaise is just as creamy and adding eggs completes the dish.

Yield: 6

Cooking Time:

Ingredient List:

- Kosher salt (1 tbsp.)
- Red bell pepper (1 ¼ cups)
- Celery (¼ cup, diced)
- Black pepper (½ tsp.)
- Yukon gold potatoes (2 lbs.)
- Canola mayonnaise (½ cup)
- Green onions (2 tbsp.)
- Eggs (3, hard boil and diced)

ssssssssssssssssssssssssssssssssssssssssssssssss

Methods:

1. Heat water in saucepan (enough to cover potatoes) along with 2 tsp. salt. Add potatoes to pan. Cook for 25 minutes or more until tender. Remove from heat, drain, rinse with cold water and put aside.

2. Drain again, cool and cut into cubes.

3. Combine potatoes with all remaining ingredients and toss to combine.

4. Chill and serve.

3) Curried Potato Salad

This potato has an interesting blend of flavors and textures. The curry adds heat while the yogurt gives it a creamy texture and added cashews for crunch.

Yield: 8

Cooking Time: 90 minutes

Ingredient List:

- Red Bliss potatoes (2 lbs., peeled and cubed)
- Curry powder (2 tsp.)
- Salt (¾ tsp.)
- Green onions (½ cup, sliced thin)
- Unsalted Cashews (2 tbsp., chopped)
- Greek yogurt (¾ cup, plain)
- Hot pepper sauce (1 ½ tsp.)
- Carrots (¾ cup, shredded)
- Celery (1/3 cup, sliced thin)

sssssssssssssssssssssssssssssssssssssssssssssssss

Methods:

1. Heat water in saucepan (enough to cover potatoes). Cube potatoes and add to pan. Cook for 10 minutes or more until tender. Remove from heat, drain and put aside.

2. Put yogurt, hot sauce, salt and curry powder in a bowl and whisk to combine.

3. Put potatoes into a bowl along with 5 tbsp. onions, yogurt blend, carrots and celery; toss to combine.

4. Top with cashews and leftover onions.

5. Chill and serve.

4) Lemon Herb Potato Salad

This potato salad will certainly stand out in whatever setting you share it. It is made with fresh herbs, lemon, olives and peppery arugula. The combination of flavors will have people requesting seconds and talking about how good it is.

Yield: 6

Cooking Time: 20 minutes

Ingredient List:

- Fingerling potatoes (¾ lb.)
- Lemon zest (¼ tsp., grated)
- Dijon mustard (1 tsp.)
- Arugula (1/3 cup, chopped)
- Parsley (1 tbsp., chopped)
- Chives (1 tbsp., chopped)
- Olive oil (1 tbsp.)
- Lemon juice (1 tbsp.)
- Pepper (¼ tsp.)
- Kalamata olives (2 tbsp., sliced)
- Basil (1 tbsp., chopped)

sss

Methods:

1. Heat water in saucepan (enough to cover potatoes). Cube potatoes and add to pan. Cook for 5 minutes or more until tender. Remove from heat, drain and put aside.

2. Combine lemon zest, mustard, oil, pepper and lemon juice in a bowl.

3. Add olives, basil, arugula, chives and parsley to mixture and stir to combine then add potatoes and toss.

5) Lemon Garlic Potato Salad

By mixing sweet potatoes with Yukon potatoes we had a twist on traditional potato salad. The potatoes are coated with simple mustard dressing in this mayo-less entrée.

Yield: 8

Cooking Time: 90 minutes

Ingredient List:

- Yukon gold potatoes (1 ½ lbs.)
- Olive oil (2/3 cup)
- Lemon juice (¼ cup)
- Dijon mustard (1 tbsp.)
- Black pepper (¾ tsp.)
- Basil (¼ cup, chopped)
- Sweet potatoes (1 ½ lbs.)
- Lemon zest (2 tsp.)
- Garlic (3 cloves, diced)
- Salt (1 tsp.)
- Pecans (½ cup, roasted and lightly salted-chopped)

ssssssssssssssssssssssssssssssssssssssssssssssssss

Methods:

1. Heat water in saucepan (enough to cover potatoes); add potatoes along with salt to pan. Cook for 30 minutes or more until tender. Drain potatoes and put aside for 20 minutes to cool.

2. Combine oil, zest, lemon juice, garlic, mustard, salt and pepper in a bowl and put aside for 30 minutes.

3. Remove peel from potatoes and slice. Put into a baking dish in rows alternating potatoes. Pour dressing on top of potatoes and top with bail and pecans.

6) German Style Potato Salad

If you are looking for a quick potato salad then this is definitely one you will want to try. Simple ingredients produce bold flavors and in less than 30 minutes you have a scrumptious side dish.

Yield: 6

Cooking Time: 20 minutes

Ingredient List:

- Fingerling potatoes (¾ lb.)
- Olive oil (1 tbsp.)
- Garlic (1 tsp., diced)
- Cider vinegar (3 tbsp.)
- Kosher salt (1/8 tsp.)
- Center cut bacon (2 slices)
- Brown sugar (2 tsp.)
- Dijon mustard (2 tsp.)
- Black pepper (¼ tsp.)
- Scallions (1/3 cup, chopped)

sssssssssssssssssssssssssssssssssssssssssssssss

Methods:

1. Heat water in saucepan (enough to cover potatoes). Cube potatoes and add to pan. Cook for 5 minutes or more until tender. Remove from heat, drain and put aside.

2. Heat skillet and cook bacon until crispy, remove bacon from skillet and crumble. Put oil into skillet and heat then add garlic, mustard and sugar, stir to combine and cook for 1minute then add vinegar.

3. Take from heat and add salt and pepper; stir to combine then add potatoes and onions.

4. Serve topped with crumbled bacon.

7) Pennsylvania Dutch Potato Salad

This potato salad is sweet and tart with a nice flavor from bacon drippings to balance the flavors. You can serve this salad either warm or chilled.

Yield: 8

Cooking Time: 40 minutes

Ingredient List:

- Yukon gold potatoes (2 ¾ lbs.)
- Celery (½ cup)
- Eggs (2, hard boiled and chopped)
- Sugar (½ cup)
- White vinegar (¼ cup)
- Kosher salt (½ tsp.)
- Dry mustard (¼ tsp.)
- Parsley (3 tbsp., chopped)
- Onion (2 cups, chopped)
- Carrot (½ cup, shredded)
- Bacon (3 slices, Applewood smoked, minced)
- Water (½ cup)
- Cider vinegar (2 tbsp.)
- Black pepper (½ tsp.)
- Eggs (2, beaten)

ssssssssssssssssssssssssssssssssssssssssssssssss

Methods:

1. Heat water in saucepan (enough to cover potatoes); add potatoes to pan. Cook for 15 minutes or more until tender. Remove from heat, drain and put aside for 10 minutes. When potatoes have cooled, remove peel and chop.

2. Put into bowl along with celery, eggs, onion and carrot; toss to combine.

3. Heat skillet and cook bacon until crisp. Take from pan leaving 2 tbsp. drippings in skillet.

4. Add water, vinegars, salt, black pepper, eggs and mustard along with sugar to pan and whisk to combine. Cook for 8 minutes until mixture thickens.

5. Pour over potatoes and stir to combine then add parsley and bacon. Toss and serve.

8) Veggie Potato Salad

This potato salad is made more filling by adding vegetables. It can be eaten alone or paired with your preferred meat for a complete meal. This is a great way to get the kids to have and enjoy their veggies.

Yield: 7

Cooking Time: 2 hours 30 minutes

Ingredient List:

- Red potatoes (2 ½ lbs., cubed)
- Olive oil (1 tbsp.)
- Sour cream (¼ cup, low fat)
- Dijon mustard (1 tbsp.)
- Celery (½ cup, chopped)
- Green beans (½ cup, steamed)
- Lemon zest (1 tbsp.)
- Black pepper
- Apple cider vinegar (2 tbsp.)
- Buttermilk (½ cup, whole)
- Mayonnaise (¼ cup, made with olive oil)
- Carrots (2, grated)
- Radishes (½ cup, sliced)
- Parsley (¼ cup, diced)
- Garlic (1 clove, diced)
- Salt

SSSSSSSSSSSSSSSSSSSSSSSSSSSSSSSSSSSSSSSSSSSSSSSSS

Methods:

1. Heat water in saucepan (enough to cover potatoes); add potatoes along with salt to pan. Cook for 5 minutes or more until tender. Drain potatoes and put into a large bowl with oil and vinegar. Toss and put aside for an hour until cool.

2. Combine buttermilk, mayonnaise, sour cream and mustard then add all remaining ingredients and add to potatoes. Toss to combine.

3. Cover and refrigerate for an hour or overnight.

9) Sour Cream Dill Potato Salad

This creamy salad is an American favorite. Greek yogurt and sour cream make a creamy base for the potatoes with dill and cucumber to seal the deal. You get traditional taste without the extra fat.

Yield: 6

Cooking Time: 20 minutes

Ingredient List:

- Fingerling potatoes (¾ lb.)
- Sour cream (2 tbsp., low fat)
- Fresh dill (1 ½ tsp., chopped)
- Black pepper (¼ tsp.)
- English cucumber (½ cup, chopped)
- Greek yogurt (1 ½ tbsp., fat free)
- Kosher salt (¼ tsp.)

sssssssssssssssssssssssssssssssssssssssssssssssssss

Methods:

1. Heat water in saucepan (enough to cover potatoes). Cube potatoes and add to pan. Cook for 5 minutes or more until tender. Remove from heat, drain and put aside.

2. Put cucumber, yogurt, pepper, sour cream and dill in a bowl and combine thoroughly.

3. Add potatoes to mixture and toss until combine.

4. Cool and serve.

10) Italian Potato Salad

Enjoy potato salad with the fattening mayonnaise. This Italian inspired side dish is crispy and delicious. The sweet and sour dressing and salami add dimension to the dish.

Yield: 6-8

Cooking Time: 55 minutes

Ingredient List:

- Fingerling potatoes (2 lbs.)
- Garlic (2 cloves)
- Olive oil (¼ cup)
- Salami (2 oz., cut into strips)
- Red wine vinegar (3 tbsp.)
- Honey (2 tsp.)
- Olive oil (1/3 cup)
- Tarragon (1 tbsp., chopped)
- Rosemary sprigs (3)
- Bay leaves (2)
- Kosher salt (2 tsp.)
- Shallot (2 tbsp., chopped)
- Dijon mustard (1 tbsp.)
- Red pepper (¼ tsp., dried and crushed)
- Baby arugula (2 cups)

ssssssssssssssssssssssssssssssssssssssssssssss

Methods:

1. Heat water in saucepan (enough to cover potatoes); add potatoes along with rosemary, bay leaves, garlic and ¼ cup oil. Cook for 15 minutes or more until tender. Drain potatoes and discard garlic, bay leaves and rosemary. Add salt, toss and put aside to cool for 10 minutes.

2. Heat skillet and cook salami until crisp then remove from pot and place on paper towels.

3. Combine shallots, vinegar, mustard, honey and red pepper using a whisk. Slowly add remaining oil and whisk until mixture is smooth.

4. Slice potatoes in half and add dressing along with tarragon and arugula. Add pepper and salt and toss.

5. Serve topped with salami.

11) Creamy Potato Salad

In this traditional potato salad we have replaced heavy mayo with a light version and yogurt to practically cut the calories in half. Each serving has only 2.5 grams of fat. Serve with grilled meats this summer and enjoy!

Yield: 6

Cooking Time: 20 minutes

Ingredient List:

- Egg (1, large)
- Mayonnaise (2 tbsp., light)
- Mustard (1 ½ tsp.)
- Red onion (3 tbsp., chopped)
- Black pepper (¼ tsp.)
- Fingerling potatoes (¾ lb.)
- Greek yogurt (1 tbsp., low fat)
- Celery (1/3 cup, chopped)
- Kosher salt (¼ tsp.)

sssssssssssssssssssssssssssssssssssssssssssssssss

Methods:

1. Heat water in saucepan (enough to cover potatoes). Cube potatoes and add to pan along with egg. Cook for 5 minutes or more until tender. Remove from heat, drain and put aside.

2. Put mayonnaise, mustard, onion. Black pepper, yogurt, celery and salt in a bowl. Stir to combine then add potatoes.

3. Remove shell from egg and chop then add to potatoes and mix together.

4. Chill and serve.

12) Greek Lamb and Potato Salad

Potatoes can be served on the side with lamb so we figured we'd put them together. Guess what? They are just as good. This potato salad can do well all on its own.

Yield: 4

Cooking Time:

Ingredient List:

- Lemon juice (¼ cup)
- Oregano (1 tsp., dried)
- Black pepper (¼ tsp.)
- Refrigerated potato wedges (20 oz.)
- Cherry Tomatoes (2 cups, cut into halves)
- Red onion (1 cup, chopped)
- Feta cheese (½ cup, crumbled)
- Honey (1 tbsp.)
- Salt (½ tsp.)
- Coriander (1/8 tsp.)
- Roasted leg of lamb (2 ¼ cups, chopped)
- Cucumber (2 cups, seeded and chopped)
- Celery (¾ cup, sliced thin)

sssssssssssssssssssssssssssssssssssssssssssssssss

Methods:

1. Mix together lemon juice, oregano, black pepper, honey, salt and coriander. Place potatoes into a large bowl and toss with half of mixture. Chill for 10 minutes.

2. Add lamb and all leftover ingredients to potatoes along with leftover dressing. Toss to combine. Chill and serve.

13) Smoked Potato Salad

The potatoes are grill and infused with flavors from mesquite wood. This smoky flavor is balanced out by adding herbs and a vinaigrette.

Yield: 6

Cooking Time: 90 minutes

Ingredient List:

- Olive oil (¼ cup)
- Kosher salt (¼ tsp.)
- Kalamata olives (1/3 cup, sliced)
- Flat leaf parsley (2 tbsp., chopped)
- Celery seed (2 tsp.)
- Black pepper (½ tsp.)
- Potatoes (1 ½ lbs., small)
- Green onions (2 stalks, sliced thin)
- Red wine vinegar (1 tbsp.)
- Dijon mustard (1 tsp.)
- Mesquite wood chips (2 cups)

sssssssssssssssssssssssssssssssssssssssssssssssssss

Methods:

1. Put wood chips into water and soak for an hour.

2. Prepare grill by lighting one side of grill to medium high and leaving one side unlit.

3. Use a knife to pierce a disposable aluminum pan and add half of wood chips; place wood chips over lit side of grill. Toss potatoes with 1 tsp. oil, pepper and salt and put into another disposable aluminum pan. Put potatoes onto unlit side of grill. Grill for 15 minutes then add leftover wood chips and grill for an additional 15 minutes.

4. Take potatoes from heat and combine with onions and olives in a bowl.

5. Mix together oil, vinegar, parsley, mustard and celery seed in a bowl and pour over potatoes. Toss to combine.

6. Chill and serve.

14) Marinated Green Bean and Potato Salad

This combination of beans and potatoes makes for a simple salad with a smoky flair.

Yield: 6

Cooking Time: 20 minutes

Ingredient List:

- Green beans (¾ lb., trimmed)
- Fingerling potatoes (½ lb., sliced vertically)
- Olive oil (1 tbsp.)
- Black pepper (½ tsp.)
- Bacon (2 slices, crumbled)
- Wax beans (½ lb., trimmed)
- White wine vinegar (¼ cup)
- Kosher salt (½ tsp.)
- Parsley (1 tbsp., diced)

sssssssssssssssssssssssssssssssssssssssssssssss

Methods:

1. Boil beans for 5 minutes and remove from heat. Drain and put into ice water; drain again and put aside.

2. Heat water in saucepan (enough to cover potatoes); add potatoes to pan. Cook for 5 minutes or more until tender. Drain potatoes and return to pan along with 2 tbsp. vinegar, heat and take from flame.

3. Mix remaining vinegar with oil, black pepper and salt. Pour over beans and toss to coat. Place beans on a dish and serve with potatoes.

4. Add parsley and bacon and serve right away.

15) Warm Potato Salad with Ramps and Bacon

This warm potato salad is truly elegant and can be served on those special occasions. It has bold flavors from ramps which have an essence of garlic and onions.

Yield: 6

Cooking Time: 70 minutes

Ingredient List:

- Potatoes (1 ½ lbs.)
- Olive oil (3 tbsp.)
- Dijon mustard (1 ½ tbsp.)
- Ramps (10)
- Salt (¼ tsp.)
- Water (3 tbsp.)
- White wine vinegar (2 tbsp.)
- Bacon (2 slices)
- Radishes (1 cup, sliced thin)
- Black pepper (¼ tsp.)

ss

Methods:

1. Set oven to 375°F.

2. Put potatoes in a baking dish and add water then use foil to cover and bake for 45 minutes or more until potatoes are tender. Remove from heat and take off foil and cool for 15 minutes. Cut into halves.

3. Combine vinegar, mustard and oil in a bowl. Heat skillet and cook bacon until crispy then remove bacon from skillet and crumble.

4. Place cut side of potatoes into skillet and cook for 5 minutes until golden. Remove from skillet and put into bowl.

5. Take roots from ramps, rinse and drain. Pat to dry and slice bulbs thinly crosswise and add to potatoes along with radishes and bacon.

6. Drizzle with dressing and add pepper and salt to taste; toss to combine.

16) Roasted Potato Salad with Mustard Dressing

This potato salad is tangy with some added sweetness from honey and sweet onions. It can be paired with steak or burgers and is best when chilled.

Yield: 8

Cooking Time: 60 minutes

Ingredient List:

- Red potatoes (3 lbs., cubed)
- Black pepper (2 tsp.)
- Bacon (2 slices, chopped)
- Garlic (2 cloves, diced)
- Mayonnaise (2 tbsp., low fat)
- Sherry vinegar (1 ½ tbsp.)
- Olive oil (1 tbsp.)
- Kosher salt (½ tsp.)
- Sweet onion (2 cups, minced)
- Dijon mustard (3 tbsp.)
- Honey (1 ½ tbsp.)

- Parsley (¼ cup, chopped)

sssssssssssssssssssssssssssssssssssssssssssssssss

Methods:

1. Set oven to 400˚F.

2. Combine potatoes with oil, black pepper and salt in a bowl. Place onto a jelly roll and bake for 40 minutes until tender. Take from heat and place into a bowl.

3. Heat skillet and cook bacon until crispy. Take from skillet reserving 1 tbsp. of drippings. Add onions to drippings and cook for 15 minutes until golden.

4. Crumbled bacon and add to potatoes along with onions. Put aside for 15 minutes.

5. Combine mayonnaise, vinegar, mustard and honey in a bowl. Add mix to potatoes and toss to combine.

17) Creamy Buttermilk Herb Potato Salad

The crème fraiche adds a light nutty and tangy flavor to the potatoes but if it is unavailable you may use sour cream. Make sure to cook the potatoes until they are tender so that they hold their shape.

Yield: 8

Cooking Time: 57 minutes

Ingredient List:

- Red potatoes (3 lbs., cut in quarters)
- Buttermilk (1/3 cup, fat free)
- Chives (2 tbsp., chopped)
- Kosher salt (1 ¼ tsp.)
- Garlic (1 clove, diced)
- Crème fraiche/sour cream (½ cup)
- Parsley (¼ cup, chopped)
- Fresh dill (1 tbsp., chopped)
- Black pepper (½ tsp.)

SS

Methods:

1. Heat water in Dutch oven (enough to cover potatoes). Cube potatoes and add to pan. Cook for 15 minutes or until tender. Remove from heat, drain and put aside to cool for half hour.

2. Put all remaining ingredients in a bowl and whisk together.

3. Add potatoes to mixture and toss.

4. Serve right away or chill before serving.

18) Herbed Potato Salad

This potato salad is bursting with French inspired flavor from white wine, tarragon and mustard. You can make it up to a day in advance.

Yield: 6

Cooking Time: 45 minutes

Ingredient List:

- Yukon gold potatoes (3 lbs.)
- White wine vinegar (3 tbsp.)
- Dijon mustard (1 tbsp., whole-grain)
- Black pepper (¾ tsp.)
- Chives (½ cup, sliced thin)
- Tarragon (1 tsp., chopped)
- White wine (1 cup, dry)
- Olive oil (2 tbsp.)
- Salt (¾ tsp.)
- Garlic (2 cloves, diced)
- Parsley (2 tbsp., chopped)

sssssssssssssssssssssssssssssssssssssssssssssssss

Methods:

1. Heat water in saucepan (enough to cover potatoes); add potatoes to pan. Cook for 20 minutes or more until tender. Drain and put aside to cool for 10 minutes. Slice potatoes into cubes and put into large bowl.

2. Bring wine to a boil in a saucepan, lower heat and simmer for 6 minutes until reduced to about ½ cup. Take from heat and pour into a bowl along with oil, salt, garlic, vinegar, mustard and black pepper. Use a whisk to combine and pour over potatoes.

3. Add tarragon, parsley and chives. Toss to combine and serve. (May be chilled before serving if you prefer).

19) Lemon Arugula Potato Salad

Make this potato salad ahead and toss with arugula right before serving. This potato salad can be paired with just about any entrée and is sure to please.

Yield: 6

Cooking Time: 25 minutes

Ingredient List:

- Yukon gold potatoes (2 lbs., peeled and cubed)
- Shallots (½ cup, diced)
- Ground mustard (2 tsp.)
- Lemon juice (1 tsp.)
- Black pepper (¼ tsp.)
- Olive oil (7 tsp.)
- Sherry vinegar (1 ½ tbsp.)
- Lemon zest (1 tsp.)
- Arugula (2 ½ cups)
- Salt (3/8 tsp.)

sss

Methods:

1. Heat water in saucepan (enough to cover potatoes). Cube potatoes and add to pan. Cook for 10 minutes or more until tender. Remove from heat, drain and put aside.

2. Heat 1 tsp. oil in a skillet and sauté shallots for 3 minutes until slightly golden. Take from flame, put into a bowl and combine with mustard, lemon juice, black pepper, vinegar, zest and salt.

3. Add leftover oil and combine then add potatoes and toss.

4. Cool and toss with arugula before serving.

20) Light and Fresh Potato Salad

If you like potato salad but really prefer not having mayonnaise then this salad is great for you. Add the vinaigrette while the potatoes are still hot so that the flavors infuse deep into the potatoes.

Yield: 12

Cooking Time:

Ingredient List:

For dressing:

- Rice vinegar (¼ cup, seasoned)
- Salt (¼ tsp.)
- Canola oil (2 tbsp.)
- Black pepper (1/8 tsp.)

For Salad:

- Red potato (5 cups, cubed)
- Cherry tomatoes (¾ cup, sliced)
- Bell peppers (¾ cup, orange-chopped)
- Canned olives (2 ¼ oz., ripe, sliced)
- Salt (½ tsp.)
- Bell pepper (¾ cup, green, chopped)
- Cucumber (1 cup, peeled and chopped)
- Green onions (¼ cup, chopped)

ssssssssssssssssssssssssssssssssssssssssssssssss

Methods:

1. Combine ingredients for dressing in a bowl using a whisk.

2. Heat water in saucepan (enough to cover potatoes); add potatoes along with ½ tsp. salt to pan. Cook for 10 minutes or more until tender. Drain and add to dressing.

3. Toss to combine, cover and set aside for 15 minutes.

4. Add cucumber along with remaining ingredients and stir gently.

5. Refrigerate until chilled and serve!

21) Farmers Market Potato Salad

Use red, brown and purple potatoes to make a colorful dish that is both attractive and mouthwatering. It can be had warm or chilled.

Yield: 6

Cooking Time: 45 minutes

Ingredient List:

- Fresh corn kernels (1 cup)
- Olive oil (2 ½ tbsp.)
- Cider vinegar (2 tbsp.)
- Tabasco sauce (½ tsp.)
- Black pepper (½ tsp.)
- Red onion (¾ cup, sliced vertically)
- Cherry tomatoes (1 cup, halved)
- Fingerling potatoes (2 lbs.)
- Tarragon (2 tbsp., chopped)
- Dijon mustard (2 tbsp., whole grain)
- Salt (¾ tsp.)

- Zucchini (¾ cup, diced)
- Cooking spray

sssssssssssssssssssssssssssssssssssssssssssssssssss

Methods:

1. Set oven to 425°F.

2. Put potatoes and corn into a jelly roll pan and use 1 tbsp. oil to drizzle over them. Toss to combine.

3. Bake for 30 minutes until tender. Remove from heat and place into a bowl.

4. Put tarragon, mustard, salt, vinegar, black pepper and hot sauce into a bowl and whisk to combine whilst adding leftover oil.

5. Put dressing over potatoes and corn and toss.

6. Heat skillet and coat with cooking spray then sauté zucchini and onion for 4 minutes until slightly golden. Add to potatoes along with tomatoes. Toss and serve.

22) Warm Potato and Goat Cheese Salad

Sour cream and goat cheese create a creamy base for this salad so no need to even miss the mayonnaise. This may not be your everyday salad but it will sure be appreciated at your next barbecue.

Yield: 12

Cooking Time: 20 minutes

Ingredient List:

- Yukon gold potatoes (2 ½ lbs., peeled and cubed)
- Salt (½ tsp.)
- Onion (1/3 cup, diced)
- Goat cheese (3 oz. pack)
- Sour cream (¼ cup, light)
- Tarragon (2 tbsp., chopped)
- Dijon mustard (1 tsp.)
- White wine (¼ cup, dry)
- Black pepper (½ tsp.)
- Flat leaf parsley (½ cup)

- Fromage Blanc (½ cup, goat milk)
- Red wine vinegar (¼ cup)
- Olive oil (2 tbsp.)
- Garlic (1 clove, diced)

sssssssssssssssssssssssssssssssssssssssssssssssss

Methods:

1. Heat water in saucepan (enough to cover potatoes); add potatoes to pan. Cook for 10 minutes or more until tender. Drain and put aside in a large bowl.

2. Combine potatoes with wine, pepper and salt; toss to combine.

3. Put in parsley, cheese and onion and combine. Combine fromage blanc with leftover ingredients and whisk thoroughly. Add mixture to potatoes and toss.

4. Serve and enjoy!

23) Lemongrass and Ginger Potato Salad

Lemongrass and ginger aren't usually what you find in potato salads but this invigorating blend makes this dish very unique.

Yield: 6

Cooking Time: 32 minutes

Ingredient List:

- Red potatoes (2 lbs., cubed)
- Sesame oil (1 ½ tbsp., dark)
- Water (1 tbsp.)
- Salt (¾ tsp.)
- Green onions (1/3 cup, sliced thin)
- Rice vinegar (2 tbsp.)
- Lemongrass (4 tsp., diced, fresh)
- Ginger (2 tsp., peeled and grated)
- Jalapeno pepper (1, diced)
- Cilantro (2 tbsp., chopped)

ss

Methods:

1. Heat water in saucepan (enough to cover potatoes). Cube potatoes and add to pan. Cook for 10 minutes or more until tender. Remove from heat, drain and put aside.

2. Put vinegar, oil, water, ginger, salt, lemongrass and jalapeno in a bowl and whisk thoroughly.

3. Add potatoes to mixture and toss to combine. Chill then add cilantro and green onions; toss to combine.

4. Serve and enjoy!

24) Potato, Chicken and Fresh Pea Salad

This potato salad is great on its own because of the addition of chicken and vegetables. Use your preferred type of chicken and take leftovers for lunch the day after and it will be just as good or maybe even better.

Yield: 4

Cooking Time: 15 minutes

Ingredient List:

- Fingerling potatoes (1 lb., cut into 1" pieces)
- Rotisserie chicken breast (2 cups, chopped)
- Red onion (½ cup, diced)
- White wine vinegar (2 tbsp.)
- Dijon mustard (1 tbsp.)
- Salt (1 tsp.)
- Garlic (1 clove, diced)
- Sugar snap peas (2 cups, fresh)
- Red bell pepper (½ cup, diced)
- Olive oil (2 tbsp.)

- Lemon juice (1 tbsp.)
- Tarragon (1 tsp., diced)
- Black pepper (½ tsp.)

sssssssssssssssssssssssssssssssssssssssssssssss

Methods:

1. Heat water in saucepan (enough to cover potatoes); add potatoes to pan. Cook for 10 minutes or more until tender then add peas and cook for an additional 2 minutes. Drain and put aside in a large bowl along with bell pepper, onion and chicken.

2. Combine oil, lemon juice, tarragon, black pepper, vinegar, mustard, salt and garlic using a whisk. Pour over potatoes and toss.

3. Chill and serve.

25) Potato Salad with Herbs and Grilled Summer Squash

The small pickles (cornichons) used in this potato salad are of French origin but you can replace them with gherkins or capers. Make this potato salad at least 2 hours ahead before serving.

Yield: 6

Cooking Time: 30 minutes

Ingredient List:

For salad:

- Red potatoes (2 lbs., small)
- Cooking spray
- Black pepper (1/8 tsp.)
- Yellow squash (¾ lb., sliced vertically)
- Kosher salt (¼ tsp.)

For dressing:

- Chives (1/3 cup, chopped)
- Basil (2 tbsp., chopped)
- Lemon zest (¼ tsp., grated)
- Water (2 tbsp.)
- Cornichons (2 tbsp., diced)
- Black pepper (1/8 tsp.)
- Parsley (3 tbsp., chopped)
- Tarragon (1 tbsp., chopped)
- Lemon juice (3 tbsp.)
- Olive oil (2 tbsp.)
- Kosher salt (¼ tsp.)

sssssssssssssssssssssssssssssssssssssssssssssss

Methods:

1. Set grill on medium heat.

5. Prepare salad by heating water in saucepan (enough to cover potatoes). Add potatoes to pan. Cook for 18 minutes or more until tender. Remove from heat, drain, cut in quarters and put aside.

2. Use cooking spray to coat squash and toss with pepper and salt. Grill for 2 minutes on both sides until golden and tender. Take from grill and to potatoes.

3. Combine all ingredients for dressing in a small bowl. Pour over potato and squash blend and toss to combine.

4. Serve right away or chill before serving.

About the Author

Allie Allen developed her passion for the culinary arts at the tender age of five when she would help her mother cook for their large family of 8. Even back then, her family knew this would be more than a hobby for the young Allie and when she graduated from high school, she applied to cooking school in London. It had always been a dream of the young chef to study with some of Europe's best and she made it happen by attending the Chef Academy of London.

After graduation, Allie decided to bring her skills back to North America and open up her own restaurant. After 10 successful years as head chef and owner, she decided to sell her business and pursue other career avenues. This monumental decision led Allie to her true calling, teaching. She also started to write e-books for her students to study at home for practice. She is now the proud author of several e-books and gives private and semi-private cooking lessons to a range of students at all levels of experience.

Stay tuned for more from this dynamic chef and teacher when she releases more informative e-books on cooking and baking in the near future. Her work is infused with stores and anecdotes you will love!

Author's Afterthoughts

I can't tell you how grateful I am that you decided to read my book. My most heartfelt thanks that you took time out of your life to choose my work and I hope you find benefit within these pages.

There are so many books available today that offer similar content so that makes it even more humbling that you decided to buying mine.

Tell me what you thought! I am eager to hear your opinion and ideas on what you read as are others who are looking for a good book to buy. Leave a review on Amazon.com so others can benefit from your wisdom!

With much thanks,

Allie Allen